S0-ANG-258

Marine Mammals

MANATEES

ZELDA KING

PowerKiDS press™

New York

Published in 2012 by The Rosen Publishing Group, Inc.
29 East 21st Street, New York, NY 10010

First Edition

Editor: Joanne Randolph
Book Design: Julio Gil

Photo Credits: Cover, pp. 9, 10 (top), 12, 13, 16, 17 Brian J. Skerry/National Geographic/Getty Images; pp. 4–5 Carol Grant/Flickr/Getty Images; p. 6 (top) Raul Touzon/National Geographic/Getty Images; pp. 6 (bottom), 8 (top), 11, 15, 22 Shutterstock.com; pp. 8 (bottom), 10 (bottom) iStockphoto/Thinkstock; p. 14 Jupiterimages/Photos.com/Thinkstock; pp. 18–19 Jeff Rotman/Iconica/Getty Images; pp. 20, 21 Jeff Foott/Discovery Channel Images/Getty Images.

Library of Congress Cataloging-in-Publication Data

King, Zelda.
  Manatees / by Zelda King. — 1st ed.
     p. cm. — (Marine mammals)
  Includes index.
  ISBN 978-1-4488-5002-0 (library binding) — ISBN 978-1-4488-5135-5 (pbk.) — ISBN 978-1-4488-5136-2 (6-pack)
  1. Manatees—Juvenile literature. I. Title.
  QL737.S63K56 2012
  599.55—dc22
                                            2010050092

Manufactured in the United States of America

CPSIA Compliance Information: Batch #WS11PK: For Further Information contact Rosen Publishing, New York, New York at 1-800-237-9932

CONTENTS

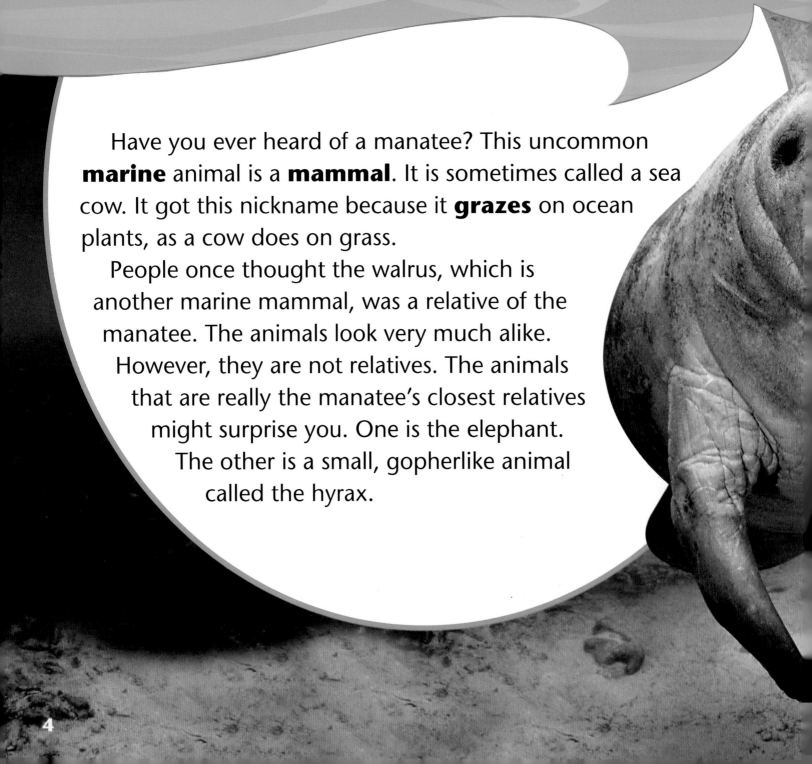

Meet the Manatee

Have you ever heard of a manatee? This uncommon **marine** animal is a **mammal**. It is sometimes called a sea cow. It got this nickname because it **grazes** on ocean plants, as a cow does on grass.

People once thought the walrus, which is another marine mammal, was a relative of the manatee. The animals look very much alike. However, they are not relatives. The animals that are really the manatee's closest relatives might surprise you. One is the elephant. The other is a small, gopherlike animal called the hyrax.

Here a manatee mother and her baby swim in the warm waters of Kings Bay, in Crystal River, Florida. About 400 manatees come to stay in Kings Bay each winter.

Warm Waters

Would you like to see a wild manatee? Then Florida is a good place to visit. Manatees like to swim in the warm, **shallow** water off Florida's coast. In the summer, they may swim in waters as far west as Texas. They can often be seen as far north as South Carolina in warm months, too. Manatees like the warm water

Above: This manatee swims in Florida's Everglades, which is a huge swampy wetland. *Right*: Manatees are big, but they do not have a lot of body fat. This means they cannot live in cold water.

Where Manatees Live

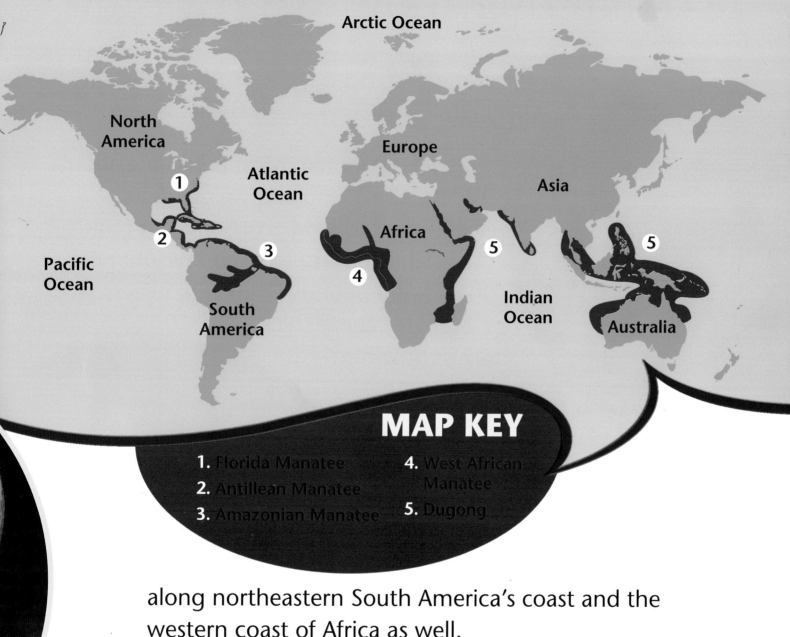

Arctic Ocean

North America

Atlantic Ocean

Europe

Asia

Africa

Pacific Ocean

South America

Indian Ocean

Australia

1

2

3

4

5

5

MAP KEY

1. Florida Manatee
2. Antillean Manatee
3. Amazonian Manatee
4. West African Manatee
5. Dugong

along northeastern South America's coast and the western coast of Africa as well.

Most ocean animals can live only in salt water. Manatees are special. Manatees can also live in freshwater. Manatees often swim up rivers looking for food.

Manatees are big. Most adults are about 10 feet (3 m) long and weigh about 1,000 pounds (454 kg). Some are more than 13 feet (4 m) long and weigh more than 3,500 pounds (1,600 kg).

Manatees have thick gray or brownish gray skin with some hair on it.

Above: This manatee is using its prehensile lips to pull plants from the ocean floor. *Right*: Scientists have discovered that manatees' whiskers are very sensitive. This means that each whisker can feel well.

Manatees have rounded tails. They use their flippers and tails to move slowly through their watery homes looking for food.

They have small eyes and big noses. Their lips are covered with thick hairs. Their lips are **prehensile**, like the end of an elephant's trunk. Manatees have two **flippers** and a wide, flat tail.

What Makes the Manatee a Mammal?

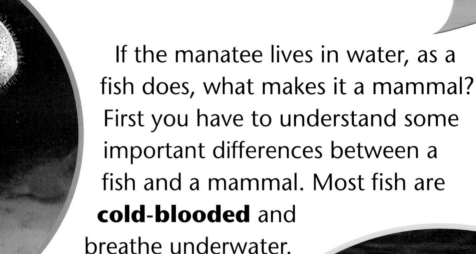

If the manatee lives in water, as a fish does, what makes it a mammal? First you have to understand some important differences between a fish and a mammal. Most fish are **cold-blooded** and breathe underwater. A mammal is **warm-blooded** and has a backbone and hair, breathes air, and

Above: One of the things that makes manatees mammals is their hair. The most noticeable hairs on a manatee are its whiskers. *Right*: Manatees can hold their breath while eating and looking for food. They need to come up to breathe air, though.

Like all mammals, manatee mothers care for their young and feed them milk. Manatees generally have one baby at a time.

feeds milk to its young. Dogs, cats, and cows are mammals. People are mammals, too!

The manatee has a backbone and hair. It cannot breathe underwater but must come up to the top for air. A mother manatee feeds her baby, or calf, milk from her body. All these things mean a manatee is a mammal, just as you are!

A Manatee's Meal

Do you like to eat vegetables? Manatees do! They are herbivores, or plant eaters. Manatees eat more than 60 kinds of plants. They like manatee grass, turtle grass, water lettuce, and all sorts of other water plants. Manatees get some of the water they need from the plants they eat. For the rest of it, they must swim to freshwater every one to two weeks to take a drink.

The thick hairs on the manatee's lips help it

This manatee is looking for food in the Weeki Wachi River, in Florida.

find the plants it likes. The manatee uses its prehensile lips and flippers to get food into its mouth.

These manatees are eating lettuce and other plant matter in their home in Homosassa Springs State Park, in Florida. These manatees do not live in the wild.

13

The Manatee's Special Teeth

Open your mouth and look at your teeth in a mirror. You have different kinds of teeth. In front of your mouth are teeth with sharp edges for biting and cutting. In back are wide, flat teeth called molars. They are for chewing.

Manatees have no front teeth. They have only molars. The ones nearest the front are the oldest. When they get worn, they fall out. However, the manatee has a special way to fill the empty spaces. The teeth behind move up.

Manatees do not have teeth in the front of their mouths, they just have tough gums, which you can see here.

The new teeth then come in at the back of the manatee's mouth. This happens over and over throughout the manatee's life!

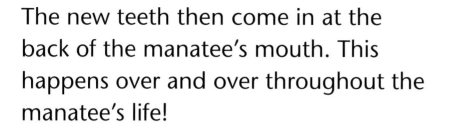

Did You Know?

A relative of the manatee called the Steller's sea cow liked cold water. It lived near Alaska. Hunters had killed all Steller's sea cows by 1768.

Life in the Slow Lane

Manatees take it easy and move slowly. They mostly swim less than 5 miles per hour (8 km/h), although they can go much faster if needed.

Besides the 6 to 8 hours a day they spend eating, manatees spend 2 to 12 hours a day resting. They also **migrate** with the seasons and in search of food.

Manatees mostly live alone, but they sometimes spend time with other manatees.

Here are two manatees spending some time together in Crystal Springs, Florida. Crystal Springs is one place to which manatees migrate in colder weather.

They talk to each other with different sounds. Just as people enjoy hugging each other, manatees enjoy touching each other. They like to play, too. They ride waves and roll around!

Manatees sometimes come together in large groups like this. Sometimes they stop looking for food and play together, too.

The Life of a Manatee

Did you know that a manatee can live about 60 years? Its life starts underwater. A newborn calf is about your size! It weighs about 65 pounds (30 kg) and is about 4 feet (1 m) long. Right away, the calf's mother pushes it above the water to breathe.

A calf stays with its mother for about two years. In a few more years, it is ready to have its own babies. After **mating**, a female carries her baby inside her body for about a year. It will be two to five years before she has another baby.

Fossils of animals that are likely the ancestors of manatees date back 45 million years. Modern manatees have been swimming in coastal waters for about one million years!

Manatee females are not able to have babies until they are around five years old. Males are not fully grown until they are about nine years old.

Many Dangers for Manatees

Sadly, the giant, gentle manatee faces many dangers. Every year, boats run into a large number of manatees and kill them. Sometimes manatees get caught in fishing nets and drown because they cannot come up to breathe. In some places, people hunt manatees for their meat, hides, and oil. **Pollution** and loss of **habitat** also put manatees in danger.

What makes all these problems worse is that manatees do not

The light lines on this manatee's back are scars from cuts made by a boat propeller.

reproduce often and they do not have a lot of babies at one time. Many manatees die each year, but only a few babies are born. This means the total number of manatees in the world keeps getting smaller and smaller.

Manatees cannot move fast enough to get out of the way if a boat is moving toward them. It is lucky for this manatee that the boat's propeller shown here is not moving.

Save the Manatee!

Today, many people are working to **protect** manatees. Laws have been passed and special manatee **sanctuaries** have been created. In some places, manatee hunting has ended. People study manatees to find the best ways to protect them. People who study manatees also teach the public about them. As the public learns more, they want to do more to protect manatees.

You can help manatees, too! Tell your family and friends about them. Talk to your family or class about giving money to a group that protects manatees. Do not let these wonderful animals disappear forever.

CAUTION

MANATEE AREA

Signs like this one warn boaters to be careful in places where manatees like to swim. This is one way people are trying to keep manatees safe.

GLOSSARY

cold-blooded (KOHLD-bluh-did) Having a body heat that changes with the surrounding heat.

flippers (FLIH-perz) Broad, flat body parts suited for swimming.

grazes (GRAYZ-ez) Feeds on grass and other plants.

habitat (HA-buh-tat) The surroundings where an animal or a plant naturally lives.

mammal (MA-mul) A warm-blooded animal that has a backbone and hair, breathes air, and feeds milk to its young.

marine (muh-REEN) Having to do with the sea.

mating (MAYT-ing) Joining together with a male to make babies.

migrate (MY-grayt) To move from one place to another.

pollution (puh-LOO-shun) Manmade waste that harms Earth's air, land, or water.

prehensile (pree-HEN-sul) Able to grab by wrapping around.

protect (pruh-TEKT) To keep safe.

reproduce (ree-pruh-DOOS) To have babies.

sanctuaries (SANK-choo-weh-reez) Places for wild animals to live where they are protected.

shallow (SHA-loh) Not deep.

warm-blooded (WORM-bluh-did) Having a body heat that stays the same, no matter how warm or cold the surroundings are.

INDEX

WEB SITES

Due to the changing nature of Internet links, PowerKids Press has developed an online list of Web sites related to the subject of this book. This site is updated regularly. Please use this link to access the list:
www.powerkidslinks.com/marm/manatees/